Marius Rombach

An Analysis of Optimistic and Pessimistic Language in Earnings Press Releases

GRIN Publishing

Bibliographic information published by the German National Library:

The German National Library lists this publication in the National Bibliography; detailed bibliographic data are available on the Internet at http://dnb.dnb.de .

Imprint:

Copyright © 2011 GRIN Verlag GmbH
Print and binding: Books on Demand GmbH, Norderstedt Germany
ISBN: 978-3-656-04044-6

This book at GRIN:

http://www.grin.com/en/e-book/180864/an-analysis-of-optimistic-and-pessimistic-language-in-earnings-press-releases

GRIN - Your knowledge has value

Since its foundation in 1998, GRIN has specialized in publishing academic texts by students, college teachers and other academics as e-book and printed book. The website www.grin.com is an ideal platform for presenting term papers, final papers, scientific essays, dissertations and specialist books.

ALBERT-LUDWIGS-UNIVERSITÄT FREIBURG IM BREISGAU

An Analysis of Optimistic and Pessimistic Language in Earnings Press Releases

Seminar Paper

submitted to

Chair of Information Systems Research

University of Freiburg

by Marius Rombach

Contents

1. Introduction

Earnings Press releases are the ticket to publicise firm's performance. While numerous studies focus on the interpretation of numerical forms, this paper deals with the influence of optimistic and pessimistic language on firm's future performance. In addition, it contrasts different approaches to measure the tone.

A closer look especially at propose and function of narrative form will be taken in Chapter 2: Rules and best practice guidelines to publish Earnings Press releases are presented and difficulties are pointed out.

Chapter 3 is based mainly on the study *"Beyond the Numbers: An Analysis of Optimistic and Pessimistic Language in Earnings Press Releases"* published by Angela K. Davis, Jeremy M. Piger and Lisa M. Sedor. They first examined the role language plays in the credible communication of information to investors. A textual analysis approach with DICTION 5.0 is presented and Results of other studies are added.

First, the preparation of a data sample for textual analyses of the connection between language and firm performance is represented. Subsequently several accounting and financial market variables to measure firm performance are collected for each earnings press release.

Then, the technique of the dictionary-based content analysis program to categorized optimistic and pessimistic words is explained extensively. Afterwards, the pros and cons of this approach are discussed critically.

Results of the analysis like the increase in the average length of earnings press releases are evaluated. Also the descriptive data of the sample is listed. A baseline multivariate regression model verified a correlation between language usage and future firm performance. The used functions have been developed on sample data and accounting and financial market variables.

Next the market response to optimistic and pessimistic language is tested. It can be seen that an unexpected portion of optimistic and pessimistic language has a stronger influence on market returns than an expected portion.

An alternative to textual analysis techniques is the naïve Bayesian learning algorithm presented in chapter 4. By comparison with the dictionary based approach advantages and drawbacks are shown.

The excursus shows a possible application of the found connection between future firm performance and language in earnings press releases. Results of the previously introduced textual analysis are used to create a business ratio. In conclusion, Chapter 7 passes review of the paper and summarizes the results.

2. Earnings Press Releases

Press releases are a ticket to publicity and to announce firm's performance in publications. Lewis et al. characterized them as "the major news event of the season" [Mahoney and Lewis (2004)] for companies and investors, financial media, analysts and the market. After quarter-end earnings, press releases should be published as soon as practicable. Within the framework of investor relations (IR), they communicate the firm's financial performance in numeric and narrative form to [cp. FEI / NIRI earnings press releases guidelines].

The U.S. Securities and Exchange Commission (SEC) established formal financial statements and regulates the way in which firms announce defined financial measures[1]. For firms listed on New York Stock Exchange (NYSE) and National Association of Securities Dealers Automated Quotations (NASDAQ) earnings press releases are mandatory.

Apart from analyses of operating results, historical data, positive and negative factors affecting key financial indicators, an accurate earn-

---

[1] Financial Executive Institute (FEI) and National Investor Relations Institute (NIRI) published practice guidelines for earnings press releases.

ings press release should contain a realistic and truthful forecast for future quarters [cp. Trautmann and Hamilton (2003)]. "Promises of specific results, exaggerated or unwarranted claims; or [...] opinions for which there is no reasonable basis" [NYSE Rules, Rule 472] should be avoided and a Safe Harbor language is to be used.

Despite these rules, language in earnings press releases ranges from a straight forward numerical view to a quite promotional presentation of the firm's development. Also opportunistical behavior in writing press releases to delude investors is used. Therefore narrative form in disclosures is likely more difficult to analyze than the numerical form[2].

Different ways to examine the language used in earnings press releases and their influence on stock markets and future firm performance will be described in the following sections. One approach is a textual analysis with DICTION 5.0 implemented by *Davis et al.* They first examined "the role that language usage plays in the credible communication of information to investors" [Davis et al. (2006), p. 25].

3. Textual Analysis of Optimistic and Pessimistic Language

3.1 Data Sample

Davis et al.'s data sample used for textual analysis consists of earnings press releases between January 1, 1998 and December 31, 2003 published by PR Newswire[3]. Diverse accounting, financial market and textual-analysis variables, like return on assets (ROA) to identify firm performance in present and future, were collected for each file. [cp. Davis et al. (2006), p. 10]

The final data sample consists of 23,662 firm quarterly earnings press releases. The initial sample of 73,758 firm quarters was stripped of any non earnings related announcements: files with no essential data

---

[2] The numeric form in earnings press releases should be prepared under Generally Accepted Accounting Principles (GAAP).
[3] PR Newswire is hired by companies to deliver news and multimedia content.

available on COMPUSTAT[4], Center for Research in Security Prices (CRSP)[5] or Institutional Brokers' Estimate System (I/B/E/S)[6], subsamples of narrative disclosures that contain officer quotations and any observations with too large deviations for each of the financial market, accounting and textual-analysis variables. [cp. Davis et al. (2006), p. 10]

3.2 Dictionary approach with DICTION 5.0

To analyze and to receive the systematic measure of the level of optimistic and pessimistic language used in the data sample computerized textual-analysis software called DICTION 5.0 is applied. This software is a dictionary-based content analysis program which has been applied extensively to evaluate speeches of politicians, annual reports to stockholders and other business communication. [7][cp. Davis et al. (2006), p. 11-12]

The ability to identify subtle aspects of language, the systematic and reliable textual analysis techniques based on pre-existing searching rules and the feasibility to analyze a larger sample size than possible by human coding or manual reading, are the main advantages of DICTION 5.0 [cp. Davis et al. (2006), p. 12]. In addition, research subjectivity and bias could be excluded. Adding observations to the sample is feasible without disturbing the scoring process [cp. Armesto et al. (2008), p. 46].

Based on linguistic theory the program counts words previously characterized as optimistic or pessimistic. The inherent inability to provide an analysis of language in relation to the context of the particular statement is a strong limitation. A sentence like "the stock is not bad" is falsely defined as pessimistic language by a dictionary based analysis [cp. Das and Chen (2001), p 1378]. In such a case a statistical approach is suitable.[8] [cp. Davis et al. (2006), p. 12]

Common words in financial context are misclassified by dictionaries or word lists created for other disciplines [cp. Loughran and McDonald

---

[4] source for report date and accounting data.
[5] source for market data.
[6] source for analysts' forecasts.
[7] See at Hart 2000a.
[8] A prospective statistical approach is the Naïve Bayesian Learning Algorithm presented on p. 8.

(2009), p. 1][9]. Consequently, DICTION 5.0 defined three pre-existing word lists titled "Praise", "Satisfaction" and "Inspiration" as "optimism-increasing". [10] Respectively three pre-existing word lists titled "Blame", "Hardship" and "Denial" are defined as "optimism-decreasing".[11] [cp. Davis et al. (2006), p. 13]

Also several accounting and financial market variables, like return on assets to measure firm performance are collected for each earnings press release in the data sample. The table in the appendix summarizes them extensively. [cp. Davis et al. (2006), p. 13]

3.3 Descriptive Evidence

The trend of a large and steady increase in the average length of earnings press releases continued during the sample period. The median value rose from 878 words at the beginning to 1,679 words at the end of the sample period. That implies a growth of 15 words per month. [cp. Davis et al. (2006), p. 15]

Descriptive data indicates that on average 1.28 % of the words were categorized as "optimism increasing" and 0.46 % of the words as "optimism decreasing". On average 70.7 % of sample firms meet or beat analyst's forecasts. Negative earnings were reported by 25.5 % of firms. [cp. Davis et al. (2006), p. 15]

3.4 Correlation between language usage and future firm performance

To verify the connection between language usage and future firm performance a baseline multivariate regression model including fixed effects[12] for explaining future performance[13] first applied by *Core, et al.*, is

---

[9] For example words like tax or liability have a negative meaning in the Harvard Dictionary but in a financial context the only describe company operations.
[10] Examples for optimism-increasing: Praise: best, great, important; Satisfaction: comfortable, enthusiasm, satisfied; Inspiration: loyalty, productivity, quality.
[11] Examples for optimism-decreasing: Blame: adverse, bad, costly; Hardship: conflict, depressed, weakness; Denial: cannot, shouldn't, nothing.
[12] As two digit Standard Industry Classification (SIC) industry and year dummy variables.
[13] Future performance is defined as average of ROA in the following four quarters.

used by *Davis et al.*. The function to evaluate the influence between language and future firm performance is:

$$FUTROA = \beta_0 + \beta_1 ROA_i + \beta_2 \sigma_{ROA,i} + \beta_3 LOGREV_i + \beta_4 SURP_i + \beta_5 BEAT_i$$
$$+ \beta_6 LOSS_i + \sum_j \beta_7 ID_{ij} + \sum_k \beta_{8k} YEAR_{ik} + \beta_9 OPT_i + \beta_{10} PESS_i + \varepsilon_i$$

[Davis et al. (2006), p. 17].

After testing the null hypothesis[14] with the restriction $\beta_9 = \beta_{10} = 0$ the result is as follows: A higher percentage of optimistic words in earning press releases predicts a higher future firm performance. Respectively a higher percentage of pessimistic words predicts a lower future firm performance. [cp. Davis et al. (2006), p. 15]

Whether optimistic and pessimistic words have a different influence on future firm performance is checked with the restriction $\beta_9 = - \beta_{10}$. A Wald Test[15] of this restriction cannot be rejected and makes the following symmetry restriction NETOPT[16] necessary:

$$FUTROA = \beta_0 + \beta_1 ROA_i + \beta_2 \sigma_{ROA,i} + \beta_3 LOGREV_i + \beta_4 SURP_i + \beta_5 BEAT_i$$
$$+ \beta_6 LOSS_i + \sum_j \beta_7 ID_{ij} + \sum_k \beta_{8k} YEAR_{ik} + \beta_9 NETOPT_i + \varepsilon_i$$

[Davis et al. (2006), p. 18].

3.5 Market response to optimistic and pessimistic language

The market response[17] of optimistic and pessimistic language is also tested with a multivariate regression model. For a detailed description of this model see *Davis et al.* As result, the connection "between market returns and unexpected portion of optimistic and pessimistic language is substantially stronger than (...) the expected portion" [cp. Davis et al. (2006), p. 22]. For market participants the results suggest that narrative forms in earnings press releases is in addition to a numerical form, a

---

[14] The null hypothesis corresponds to a general or default position of an observed data test.
[15] The Wald test checks whether an independant variable has a conventional significance level to the baseline multivariate regression model.
[16] NETOPT defined as difference between OPT and PESS.
[17] Based on size adjusted stock returns in a three day window around the earnings press releases data.

"credible (…) source of information about managers' future earnings expectations" [cp. Davis et al. (2006), p. 22].

In addition to the previous dictionary based approaches, the statistical approaches based on statistical inference like the Naïve Bayesian Learning Algorithm with other strengths and weaknesses can be used [cp. Li (2009), p. 12]. In the next chapter this potential alternative will be explained and compared exemplary with the dictionary approach.

4. A Different approach: Naïve Bayesian learning algorithm

The Naïve Bayesian Algorithm based on Thomas Bayes[18] is the oldest and most successful natural language algorithm. Detecting web communities, classifying pages on Internet portals, the usage in spam filters and for web search algorithms are actual scopes of application. [cp. Antweiler et al. (2004), p. 1264; cp. Das et al. (2007), p.1379].

This specific statistical learning approach reduces a given sentence to a list of words. Each word is weighted and categorized into a specific class from a set of all feasible classes. To learn the required classification, manually coded sentences are used as training dataset [cp. Li (2008), p. 2-13].

The "naïve" underlying assumption that the occurrence of a word in a document is independent of every other word in the document is highly unrealistic and false.[19] However the effects on results are negligible and the advantages like a simplification of computation dominate. Also the curse of dimensionality problem[20] is avoided. [cp. Antweiler et al. (2004), p. 1264; cp. Li (2007), p.13]

According to *Li*, the Naïve Bayesian Approach seems to perform better to evaluate the influence of tone than a dictionary based approach.

---

[18] Thomas Bayes was an English mathematician of the 18th century.
[19] Words correlate with each other.
[20] the curse of dimensionality refers to the fact that some problems become intractable as the number of the variables increases.

To analyze optimistic and pessimistic language in earnings press releases the use of the Naïve Bayesian Approach should easily be possible.

Advantages by comparison to dictionary based approaches are an independency of language which enables an analysis in non-English press releases. Also prior research knowledge about text may be considered and the analysis of language can be adjusted to the context of the particular statement[21]. However, other approaches do not required manual coded sentences as training data set for categorization and have been successfully applied in other language researches. [cp. Li (2008) p. 1-33; cp. Das et al. (2007), p.1379]

5. Similar Studies

Several studies examined the narrative form of earnings announcements, chairman's report, manager's message to stockholders etc. and their effects on future firm performance and market reaction. For example readability is measured, keywords are counted and different statistical approaches are used. [Merkl-Davies and Brennan (2006), pp. 116-196]

Despite of the rather special subject area a few studies have also been conducted on the influence of tone in future firms performance. They all achieved same or similar results. Like *Davis et al.*, they often use COMPUSTAT, CRSP and IBES for data matching.

Tetlock et al. analyzed 2008 whether expectations of firms' individual stock returns can be verify with a measure of language. They examined the influence of negative words in all Dow Jones News Services (DJNS) and Wall Street Journal stories between 1980 and 2004 of S&P 500 firms. [cp. Tetlock (2008), p. 1437-1467]

One weakness in contrast to *Davis* and *Henry* is that no specific word list is used. For analyses, a textual program called General Inquirer

---

[21]No dictionary especially built for the settings of earnings press releases results is obtainable, words that are generally perceived to have a negative meaning, can receive a neutral or even positive meaning when used within a financial context.

which is based on Harvard IV dictionary is used. [cp. Tetlock (2008), pp. 1437-1467]

Their main result is that low firm earnings are forecasted by the percentage of negative words in the financial press. Another finding is that firms' stock prices react to information transported by negative language with a slight delay. When relating to future firm performance, negative words are helpful indicators of earnings and returns. [cp. Tetlock (2008), pp. 1437-1467]

In 2006 *Henry* verified an impact of tone in earnings press releases on investors' reactions to earnings. Her paper "*are investors influenced by how earnings press releases are written?*" examines inter alia[22] the tone of earnings press releases by using a frequency count of positive or negative keywords. [cp. Henry (2006), pp. 363-407]

The study is using a sample period over four years, between 1998 and 2002 and contains 1,366 firm year observations for 562 firms in tele-communications and computer industry. *Henry* also used DICTION 5.0 to categorize positive and negative keywords. [cp. Henry (2006), pp. 363-407]

The hypothesis "that tone of earnings press releases influences in-vestors' reactions to earnings" [Henry (2006), p. 363] is confirmed. *Henry* mentions as one explanation for this result the prospect theory[23] based on *Tversky and Kahneman* [cp. Kahneman and Tversky (1981), pp. 453-458].

An example for the application of a Naïve Bayesian Machine's Learning Approach is *Li's* study. In 2007, he examined the effects of tone information content of the forward-looking statements (FLS) in corporate filings. He analyzed between 1994 and 2007 about 13 million FLS from 140,000 corporate 10-Q and 10 K filings for further performance. [cp. Li (2008) p. 1-33]

---

[22] apart from the overall length, textual complexity, numerical intensity and abnormal share price returns.
[23] People value gains and losses differently. Decisions base on perceived gains rather than perceived losses.

Li calculates the tone as a function of several variables like current performance, return volatility, size etc. Firms with good variable values have the tendency for more positive FLS. Thus a positive correlation between average tone in Management's Discussion and Analysis (MD&A's) and future earnings and liquidity is a result. [cp. Li (2008) p. 1-33]

6. Excursus: A prospective business ratio

Language in earnings press releases influences the future firm performance. Several different studies draw this conclusion. The question that arises is how this knowledge could be used profitably for investors. One opportunity is to analyze the optimistic and pessimistic language of the earnings press releases of one company. A prospective theoretical approach to use this knowledge is to measure the NETOPT ratio.

6.1 The Business Ratio

DICTION 5.0 counts optimistic and pessimistic words by means of pre-generated word lists and categorizes them. Finally NETOPT ratio, the difference between optimistic and pessimistic words in percent of earnings press releases is calculated.

6.2 The Data sample

NETOPT is presented as business ratio in proportion to a comparison ratio of a control sample. This sample consists of data from the same or similar branch of business[24] and is collected during the same period. Thus an industry specific NETOPT ratio could be compare with firm's individual NETOPT ratio.

---

[24] For example telecommunications and computer industry like *Henry* used it in her sample.

6.3   The Application of NETOPT ratio

As benchmark, the NETOPT ratio could help investors rate firms and draws useable conclusions of future firm performance. In contrast to traditional business ratios created with realized figures, it is based on future earnings expectations.[25]

6.4   Flaws of NETOPT ratio.

In comparison to numerical evaluation like price-earnings ratio a narrative analysis has significant drawbacks: There are no fixed rules but only best practice guidelines established on how to publish earnings press releases. Opportunistical behavior of firms to delude investors is possible. So Firms could knowingly employ optimistic (negative) words in earnings press releases to affect their NETOPT ratio positively (negatively). Possible flaws influences on the investment decision should be counterbalanced when combined with other established business ratio.

7. Conclusions

Earnings press releases are an essential part of investor relation for firms. Several rules and best practice guidelines regulate how to publish them. The large scope of narrative form in disclosures makes them more difficult to analyze than the numerical form.

The influence of tone in earnings press releases on future firm performance is confirmed of several studies. One opportunity to measure optimistic and pessimistic language is the presented textual analysis approach with diction 5.0. Based on Davis et al. words of a data sample were categorized in previous defined word lists.

The connection between optimistic and pessimistic language and future firm performance was verified with two functions. In addition, the market response to language was tested. The results of the dictionary analysis and diverse accounting and financial market variables were used for that.

---

[25] See at 2.5 Market response to optimistic and pessimistic language

Next, as a statistical alternative, the Naïve Bayesian Learning Algorithm was introduced. Pros and Cons were compared with DICTION 5.0. Final the excursus presented a prospective application of *David et al.'s* results.

Overall an influence of optimistic and pessimistic language in earnings press releases can be verified. Several studies with same or similar analysis came to this conclusion. The industrial relevance is not as simple: The familiar problems of narrative form in earnings press releases like opportunistical behavior and insufficient rules complicate an application.

Appendix: Declaration of the Accounting and Financial Variables

VARIABLE	DECLARATION
BEAT	defined as 1 if SURP ≥ 0 and 0 otherwise
FUTROA	future performance as the average of ROA in four quarters subsequent to the current quarter
ID	two digit SIC industry dummy variable, coefficient estimates ID is omitted for presentation purposes
LOGREV	logarithm of REV as a measure of firm size.
LOSS	defined as 1 if earnings are negative and 0 otherwise.
NEG	the percent of words in the "optimism-decreasing" word lists
NETOPT	is equal to OPT-PESS
OPT	the percent of words in the "optimism-increasing" word lists
REV	current quarter COMPUSTAT sales
ROA	return on asset for the current and four subsequent quarters
	Scalar: total assets measured at the beginning of the quarter
SURP	difference between actual earnings and the most recent consensus analyst earnings forecast made prior to the earnings announcement
	Scalar: stock price at the beginning of the current quarter
YEAR	two digit SIC year dummy variable, coefficient estimates YEAR is omitted for presentation purposes
σ_{ROA}	standard deviation of ROA over the four quarters subsequent to the current quarter

The table is based on *Davis et al.*

References and reading list

Antweiler, Werner, and Murray Z. Frank, 2006, Do U.S. Stock Markets Typically Overreact to Corporate News Stories?, University of British Columbia Working Paper.

Antweiler, Werner, and Murray Z. Frank, 2004, Is All That Talk Just Noise? The Information Content of Internet Stock Message Boards, *Journal of Finance 59*, 1259-1294.

Armesto, M.T., R. Hernandez-Murillo, M. Owyang, and J. Piger, 2008, Measuring the Information Content of the Beige Book: A Mixed Data Sampling Approach, *Journal of Money, Credit and Banking.*

Bowen, R. S. Rajgopal, and M. Venkatachalam, 2005, Accounting discretion, corporate governance and firm performance. Working paper. University of Washington and Duke University.

Bowen, R., A. Davis and D. Matsumoto, 2005, Emphasis on pro forma versus GAAP earnings in quarterly press releases: Determinants, SEC intervention, and market reactions, *The Accounting Review 80*, 1011-1038.

Core, J., R. Holthausen, and D. Larcker, 1999, Corporate governance, chief executive officer compensation and firm performance. *Journal of Financial and Economics 51*: 371- 406.

Das, Sanjiv, and Mike Chen, 2001, Yahoo! for Amazon: Opinion extraction from small talk on the web, Working paper, Santa Clara University.

Davis, A., J. Piger and M. Sedor, 2006, Beyond the Numbers: An Analysis of Optimistic and Pessimistic Language in Earnings Press Releases, Federal Reserve Bank of St. Louis Working Paper.

Demers, Elizabeth, and Clara Vega, 2008, Soft information in earnings announcements: News or noise?, Working paper, INSEAD.

Engelberg, Joseph, 2008, Costly information processing: Evidence from earnings announcements, Working paper, Northwestern University.

FEI and NIRI Issue Earnings Press Release Guidance, 2001 (http://www.prnewswire.com).

Hart, R. P. 2000a. DICTION 5.0: The text-analysis program. Thousand Oaks, CA: Scolari/Sage Publications.

Henry, Elaine, 2006, Are investors influenced by how earnings press releases are written?, Working paper, University of Miami.

Li, Feng, 2008, Annual report readability, current earnings, and earnings persistence, Journal of Accounting and Economics 45, 221-247.

Li, Feng, 2009, The determinants and information content of the forward-looking statements in corporate filings - a Naïve Bayesian machine learning approach, Working paper, University of Michigan.

Mahoney, W. and Lewis, J.: The IR Book, 2004 (http://www.ir-book.com/).

Mayew, William J. and Mohan Venkatachalam, 2009, The power of voice: Managerial affective states and future firm performance, Working paper, Duke University.

New York Stock Exchange Rules, 2011 (http://rules.nyse.com/nyse/).

Tetlock, Paul C., M. Saar-Tsechansky, and S. Macskassy, 2008, More than words: Quantifying language to measure firms' fundamentals, Journal of Finance 63, 1437-1467.

Trautmann, T. and J. Hamilton, 2006, Informal corporate disclosure under federal securities law: Press releases, analyst calls, and other communications, Chicago, IL: CCH Incorporated, 2006.

Tversky, A., and D. Kahneman, 1981, The framing of decisions and the psychology of choice, Science 211, 453-458.